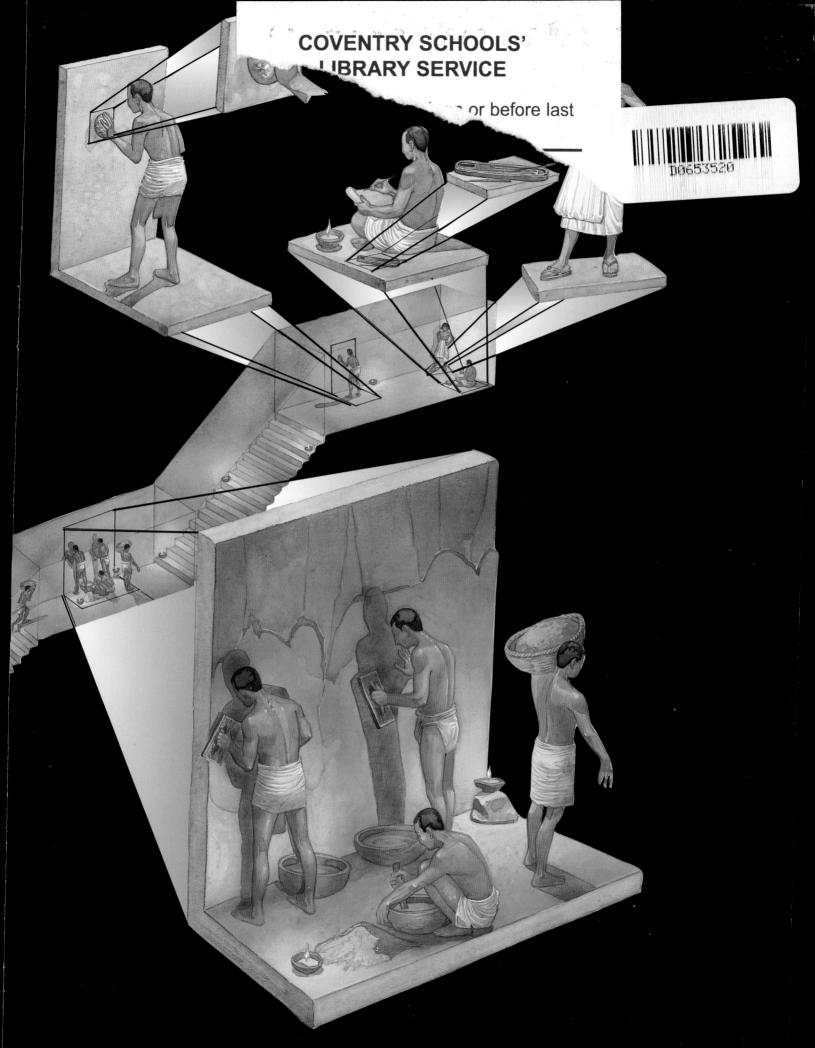

Author:

Jacqueline Morley studied English at Oxford University. She has taught English and History and has a special interest in the history of everyday life. She has written historical fiction and non-fiction for children and is the author of the award-winning *An Egyptian Pyramid* in the *Inside Story* series.

Artist:

Nick Hewetson was educated in Sussex at Brighton Technical School and studied illustration at Eastbourne College of Art. He has since illustrated a wide variety of children's books.

Additional artists: **Dave Antram, Carolyn Scrace**

Series creator:

David Salariya was born in Dundee, Scotland. In 1989 he established the Salariya Book Company. He has designed and created many new series for publishers in the UK and overseas. He lives in Brighton with his wife, the illustrator Shirley Willis, and their son Jonathan.

Editor: Editorial Assistant:
Karen Barker Smith   **Stephanie Cole**

Published in Great Britain in 2005 by Book House, an imprint of **The Salariya Book Company Ltd** 25 Marlborough Place, Brighton BN1 1UB

Please visit the Salariya Book Company at:
www.salariya.com

ISBN 1 904194 66 4

A catalogue record for this book is available from the British Library.
Printed and bound in China.

Visit our website at **www.book-house.co.uk**
for free electronic versions of:
You Wouldn't Want to Be an Egyptian Mummy!
You Wouldn't Want to Be a Roman Gladiator!
Avoid joining Shackleton's Polar Expedition!
Avoid sailing on a 19th-century Whaling Ship!

CONTENTS

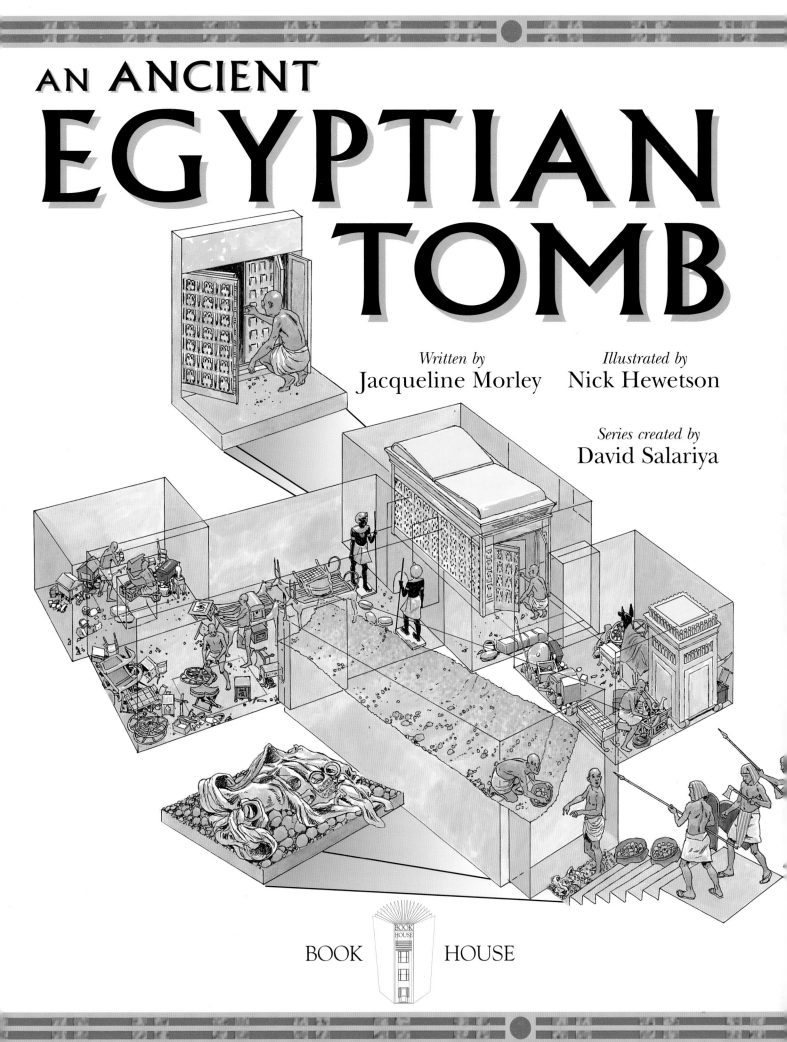

AN ANCIENT
EGYPTIAN
TOMB

Written by
Jacqueline Morley

Illustrated by
Nick Hewetson

Series created by
David Salariya

BOOK HOUSE

THE LAND OF EGYPT

THE RIVER NILE runs the whole length of Egypt. Without it, the land would just be desert, since it rarely rains. However, the Nile floods its banks yearly, providing rich soil and precious water that the ancient Egyptians carefully channelled into canals. They believed that these floods were gifts from the gods.

Each year the Nile's flood covered the river banks with fertile mud in which crops thrived. Egypt's farmland was confined to this belt of land, (green on the map left).

River Nile

Red Sea

Desert

Thebes

Valley of the Kings

The globe (left) shows Egypt's location in north east Africa.

Above, a provincial governor arrives by boat to visit the pharaoh.

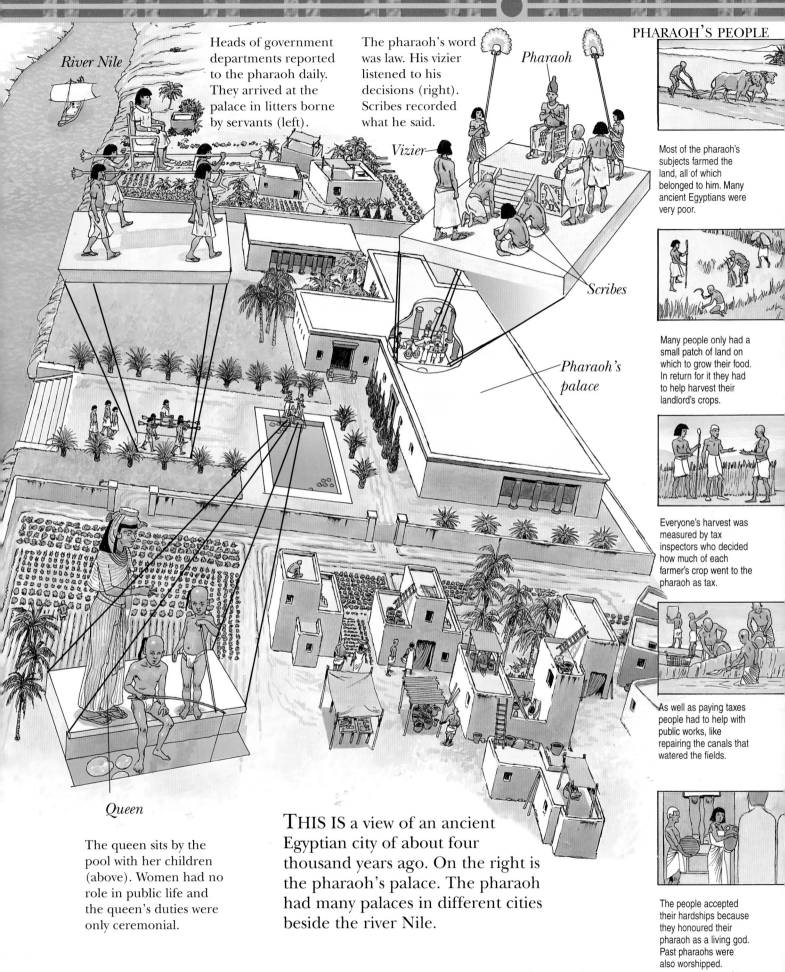

River Nile

Heads of government departments reported to the pharaoh daily. They arrived at the palace in litters borne by servants (left).

The pharaoh's word was law. His vizier listened to his decisions (right). Scribes recorded what he said.

Pharaoh

Vizier

Scribes

Pharaoh's palace

Most of the pharaoh's subjects farmed the land, all of which belonged to him. Many ancient Egyptians were very poor.

Many people only had a small patch of land on which to grow their food. In return for it they had to help harvest their landlord's crops.

Everyone's harvest was measured by tax inspectors who decided how much of each farmer's crop went to the pharaoh as tax.

As well as paying taxes people had to help with public works, like repairing the canals that watered the fields.

Queen

The queen sits by the pool with her children (above). Women had no role in public life and the queen's duties were only ceremonial.

THIS IS a view of an ancient Egyptian city of about four thousand years ago. On the right is the pharaoh's palace. The pharaoh had many palaces in different cities beside the river Nile.

The people accepted their hardships because they honoured their pharaoh as a living god. Past pharaohs were also worshipped.

7

THE MYTH OF RA

Ra, the sun god, appeared from watery nothingness and created all things by speaking their names. As he named them, they appeared.

When the sun set, people believed that Ra was beginning his nightly voyage through the underworld.

He would guide the sun's boat through the land of darkness and be born again at dawn.

When a pharaoh died, he joined his father Ra in the sun's boat. The next pharaoh became the new son of Ra on earth.

Priestesses

Priestesses, each shaking a rattle called a *sistrum*, performed sacred dances as part of the temple ritual.

Dressing the statues

Each day priests washed and dressed the statues and images of the gods in the temple and offered them food.

On a god's festival day, its image was paraded through the streets in a veiled shrine. It was too sacred for the people to gaze at directly. Below, a procession returns to the temple.

Temple —

Shrine —

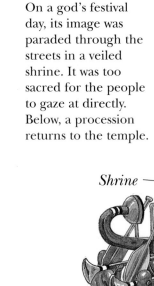

THE MYTH OF OSIRIS

Long ago, when the gods lived on earth, Ra ruled Egypt. He was succeeded by Osiris, son of Nut, the sky goddess. Osiris ruled wisely and well.

Osiris's evil brother Set plotted to kill him by offering a chest as a gift to anyone who could fit inside it. When Osiris tried, Set's henchmen nailed him in.

The chest, now Osiris's coffin, was thrown into the Nile and swept out to sea, to a far away land where a tamarisk tree enclosed it in its trunk.

Osiris's wife, Isis, went in search of him and found the chest in a pillar which the king of that land had made from the tamarisk trunk.

Incense burner

The incense burner's small container held gums and spices that produced fragrant smoke pleasing to the gods.

At the temple's innermost shrine, the pharaoh would burn incense before the chief god (left).

Beyond the pillared temple forecourt were storerooms full of offerings to the gods.

Storeroom

Pillared inner courtyard   *Side chambers*

GODS AND TEMPLES

THE PHARAOH WAS the chief priest of all the temples in Egypt and had a special relationship with the gods. His people believed that he was the son of Ra, the sun god. This explained why the gods were so generous to the Egyptians, sending them blessings like the Nile floods, which made their land prosperous. The people gave thanks by building temples for the gods and bringing them offerings of incense and food, to feed their *kas*. They believed everyone had a *ka*, which was the life-force of a person, their spiritual double. While the *ka* lived its owner would not die.

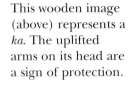

This wooden image (above) represents a *ka*. The uplifted arms on its head are a sign of protection.

She brought his body home, but the furious Set tore it into pieces which he scattered in the Nile. Isis searched the river until she had found them all.

Isis put all the pieces together and, with the help of the jackal god Anubis, who bound up Osiris's body, she brought him back to life.

Ra then made Osiris king of the underworld where he welcomed the dead whose past lives had been good. Their goodness was judged by weighing their hearts in the scales of truth. Bad hearts were heavy and were eaten by a monster who waited by the scales.

A HOUSE FOR ETERNITY

THE MYTH OF OSIRIS gave people faith in an afterlife. For the pharaoh there was a glorious future, as he would join his father Ra in the Boat of the Sun. But there could be no immortality for a person whose body decayed. The body was the home of the *ka* and without it the *ka* and its owner would die. To escape this fate, the early pharaohs built pyramids to house their bodies everlastingly. Each pyramid had what is called a 'mortuary temple' against its east face, in which priests performed the rites that kept the pharaoh's *ka* alive.

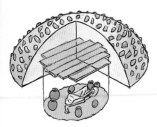

In prehistoric Egypt, a dead body was protected by a large mound of earth, which was built up over the burial pit.

In time, the mound was shaped to look like a house. It covered a stepped platform of bricks protecting a sunken burial chamber.

This ancient Egyptian image shows a *stela* (a memorial stone) on a stepped mound. The stela reads 'Protection around Horus'.

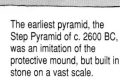

The earliest pyramid, the Step Pyramid of c. 2600 BC, was an imitation of the protective mound, but built in stone on a vast scale.

The mortuary temple contained several enormous statues, each representing the pharaoh.

Statue of pharaoh

Coffin-bearers

After the pharaoh's funeral his coffin-bearers returned along a covered causeway which linked the pyramid with a small temple.

Temple

Causeway

Causeways were brightly painted (right).

Decorated piece of wall

THE TEMPLE RITUALS

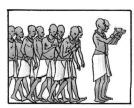

The priests of a mortuary temple were divided into groups of ten and each group was on duty in the temple for a month at a time.

The priests opened each of the temple's shrines daily, removed the linen shawl that clothed the statue within and offered it sacred oil.

The statue was then ritually washed and redressed in a new shawl. During the ceremony a 'lector' priest recited sacred verses.

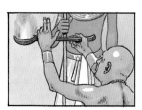

Throughout the ceremony, a purification priest carrying a censer burned sweet-smelling incense before the statue.

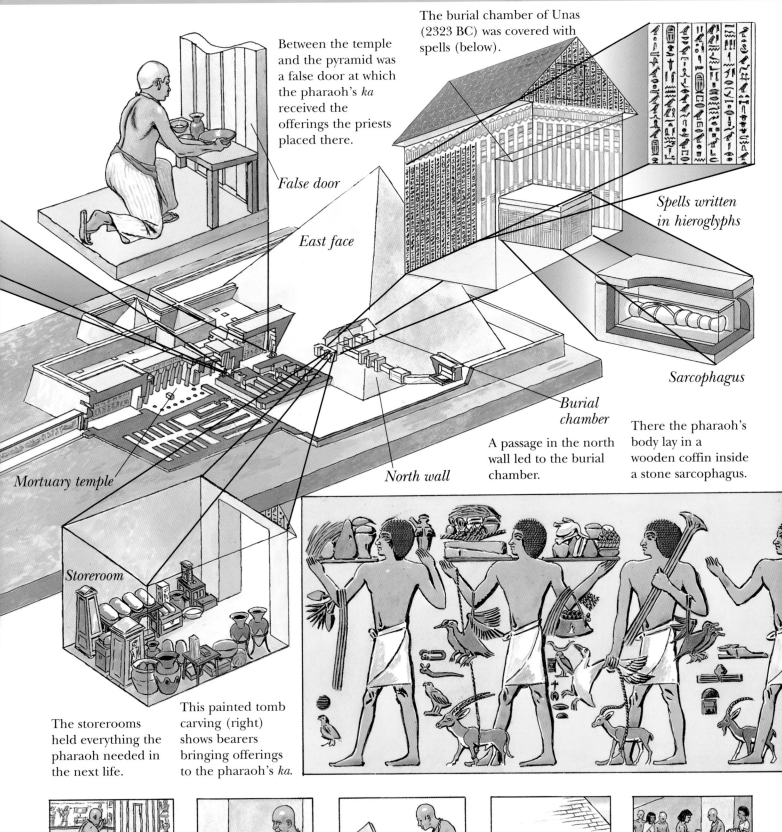

Between the temple and the pyramid was a false door at which the pharaoh's *ka* received the offerings the priests placed there.

False door

East face

The burial chamber of Unas (2323 BC) was covered with spells (below).

Spells written in hieroglyphs

Sarcophagus

Burial chamber

North wall

A passage in the north wall led to the burial chamber.

There the pharaoh's body lay in a wooden coffin inside a stone sarcophagus.

Mortuary temple

Storeroom

The storerooms held everything the pharaoh needed in the next life.

This painted tomb carving (right) shows bearers bringing offerings to the pharaoh's *ka*.

A ritual meal was then placed before the false door in the offering hall and sacred water was poured on the offering table.

This water flowed into a basin which was ceremonially emptied into an outlet running under a wall of the offering hall.

At the end of the ritual, the water vessel, basin, prayer roll and other equipment were carefully checked and replaced in chests.

Twice a day two priests walked round the pyramid clockwise (in imitation of the sun's path), sprinkling it with sacred water as they went.

Much of the food and other provisions used ceremonially were afterwards given to the 'pensioners' of the temple.

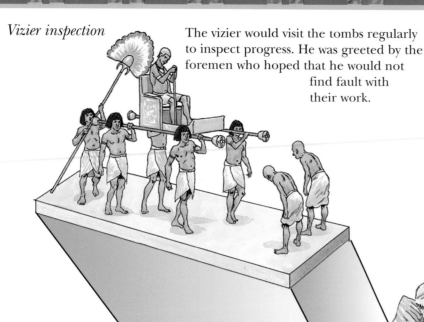

Vizier inspection

The vizier would visit the tombs regularly to inspect progress. He was greeted by the foremen who hoped that he would not find fault with their work.

All supplies, even water, had to be brought to the valley on donkeys (right).

THE VALLEY OF THE KINGS

THE RICH CONTENTS of the pyramids attracted thieves. This was probably why the New Kingdom pharaohs started to hide their burials in a remote valley opposite the city of Thebes. Here, over six centuries, the pharaohs' workmen cut deep into the hillside to create the series of magnificent royal tombs that give the valley its name. Now it is one of the world's top tourist attractions – in ancient times it was a building site with work always in progress.

DESIGNING THE TOMB

As soon as a pharaoh came to the throne he began to plan his tomb. He would order his vizier to organise it.

The vizier consulted a royal architect and they studied plans showing where existing tombs lay. They had to avoid cutting into these.

The architect travelled to the valley to check possible sites. The journey across the Nile, into the desert and up a track into the hills would have been hot and tiring. The valley was hidden from view by rocks that almost met, forming a narrow entrance that was always guarded.

One of the builders' foremen would meet the architect in the valley to offer his opinion on a likely site. A scribe noted down the foreman's advice.

The map below shows how a valley in the hills hid the tombs. Their mortuary temples lay at the foot of the hills.

Coppersmiths (below) were constantly at work casting new blades for the masons' chisels and resharpening blunt ones.

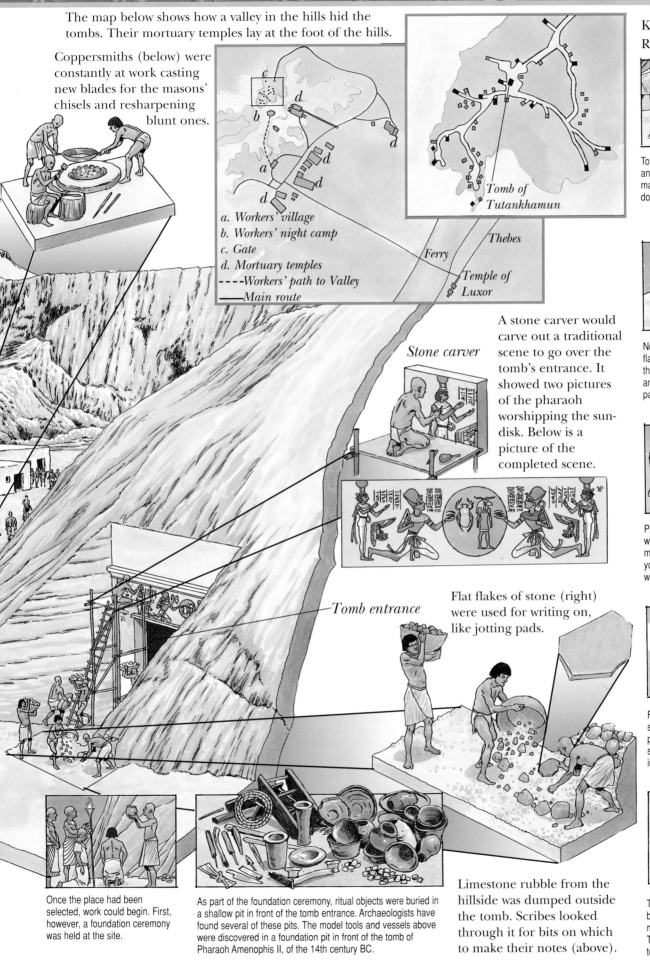

a. Workers' village
b. Workers' night camp
c. Gate
d. Mortuary temples
----Workers' path to Valley
——Main route

Tomb of Tutankhamun

Thebes

Ferry

Temple of Luxor

To keep track of the work and control costs, scribes made notes of all work done and equipment used.

Notes were made on flakes of stone, but later the scribe would write an official report on papyrus paper.

Papyrus was a reed that was plentiful in the Nile marshes. To make paper, young freshly cut stems were needed.

First the tough outer skin of the stem was peeled away. Then the soft inside pith was cut into long thin strips.

The strips were laid side by side and covered with more at right angles. They were pounded together to form a sheet.

A stone carver would carve out a traditional scene to go over the tomb's entrance. It showed two pictures of the pharaoh worshipping the sun-disk. Below is a picture of the completed scene.

Stone carver

Tomb entrance

Flat flakes of stone (right) were used for writing on, like jotting pads.

Once the place had been selected, work could begin. First, however, a foundation ceremony was held at the site.

As part of the foundation ceremony, ritual objects were buried in a shallow pit in front of the tomb entrance. Archaeologists have found several of these pits. The model tools and vessels above were discovered in a foundation pit in front of the tomb of Pharaoh Amenophis II, of the 14th century BC.

Limestone rubble from the hillside was dumped outside the tomb. Scribes looked through it for bits on which to make their notes (above).

THE TOMB BUILDERS' VILLAGE

THE TOMB WORKERS

The workers were divided into two teams, each directed by a foreman who was responsible to the vizier.

Each team also had a scribe. They recorded the work done, tools used, wages paid and sent the vizier reports.

Team size varied but it could be up to 120 men, including porters, stonemasons, sculptors, plastermakers, painters and scaffolders.

Scribe

Workers could earn extra rations if the vizier was very pleased with their work. A scribe would note down each item as it arrived.

IN A BARREN DIP in the hills to the south east of the Valley of the Kings lay a mud-brick village ringed by a wall with a single gate. An early New Kingdom pharaoh built the village to house his tomb workers and their families. Since then many generations lived there, as the job of tomb worker was often handed down from father to son. The tombs of past villagers lined the hill slope beyond the village wall.

The storekeeper was in charge of the warehouses. With him were two 'tomb guardians', who policed the warehouses.

LIFE IN THE VILLAGE

Most of the time, the men of the village were away working in the tombs. Everyday village life was run by the women. Above, a village woman supervises servants as they make flour from the village grain ration.

Fathers taught their sons their trade, in the hope that when they grew up they would also work on the royal tombs.

To get a promotion or a job for a family member, people would give the right official one or two presents.

Records reveal some jealousies and hatreds amongst the villagers. This man is dictating a letter to the vizier, accusing a rival.

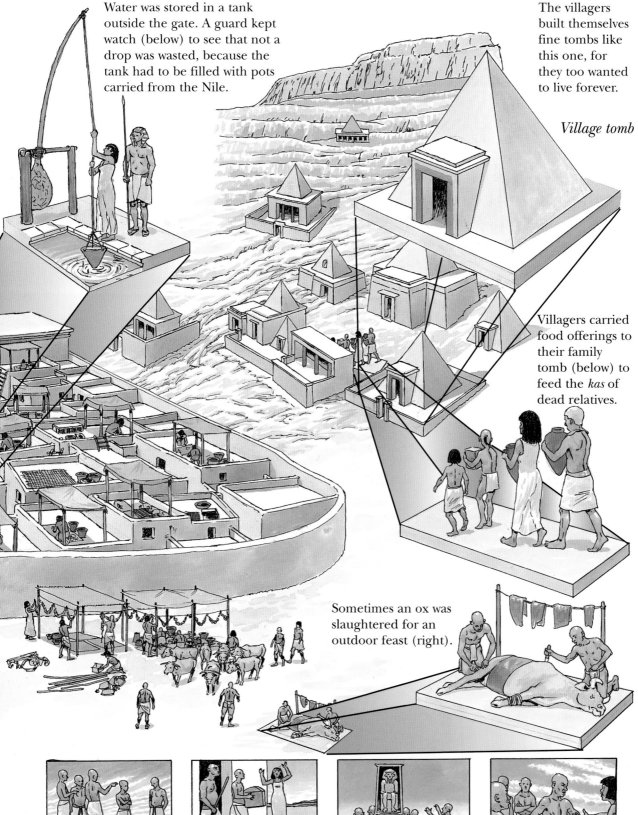

Water was stored in a tank outside the gate. A guard kept watch (below) to see that not a drop was wasted, because the tank had to be filled with pots carried from the Nile.

The villagers built themselves fine tombs like this one, for they too wanted to live forever.

Village tomb

Villagers carried food offerings to their family tomb (below) to feed the *kas* of dead relatives.

Sometimes an ox was slaughtered for an outdoor feast (right).

The village had servants and slaves to do the jobs that made life possible in such a barren and isolated place. They fetched all the supplies and water.

Servants washed the laundry in the river Nile. It was a long trip by donkey but was easier than carrying water to the village.

Servants also did shopping for the villagers, bringing back fish caught by the Nile boatmen and fresh produce from markets near the river.

Leading the village goats to grazing land was another job. Goats eat almost anything that grows but there was not much vegetation around the village.

The village had a court to deal with any crimes and disputes. It was made up of respected villagers, including the scribes and foremen.

The tomb guardians acted as court bailiffs. They confiscated the property of convicted people as payment.

At the festival of the local god, people could appeal to the statue of the god for judgement. They asked it a question and the statue appeared to nod yes or no.

In troubled times the men's wages, which were paid in food, did not always arrive. The men went on strike until they got paid.

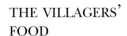
A WORKER'S HOUSE

INSIDE THE WALL, the villagers' houses were crammed together, each joined to its neighbour, along both sides of the street. They were narrow and dark, with one room leading straight to the next, but the darkness was welcome after the fierce Egyptian sun. There was not much furniture, just stools, low tables on which meals were served and chests and jars used for storage.

The owner of a house like the one below would have been well off. He had a bed (many people slept on mats) and his wife had a pretty toiletry box.

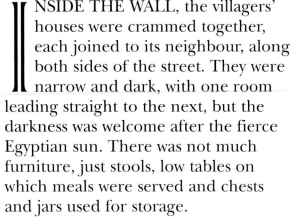

Headrest *Toiletry box*

Duck
Goose
Fish
Beans
Chick peas
Leeks
Lettuce
Radishes
Cucumber
Garlic
Bread
Olive oil
Sweet cakes
Figs
Grapes
Pomegranates

Oven

Cooking was done under a lattice roof that let the smoke escape. Right, a servant grills a goose over a brazier of charcoal.

The basic diet of all but the wealthiest ancient Egyptians was made up of bread, beans, fruit and vegetables, with some fish and very little meat. As it was impossible to grow food on the land around the village, the villagers relied on provisions to be sent to them from the pharaoh's storehouses. These supplies were their wages, as coins were not yet used.

Roofs provided extra living space. Women chatted and did their spinning there. Children played with their toys or ran from roof to roof.

When the weekend came, the children dashed down to the village gate to greet their fathers who had been away all week, working in the valley.

For relaxation after a hard week, a draughts match was a favourite pastime. The Egyptians played several other board games whose rules are now unknown.

In the game called 'Serpent', the board was shaped like a coiled snake. Players threw coloured balls to move the lion-shaped playing pieces.

Every house in the village had shrines to the gods. This home's shrine holds an image of Bes (left), a kindly god who guarded the home and the family.

Basket making

Women often took their basket making work onto the roof. Baskets were made from rushes which were wound in a coil, each row overstitched to fasten it to the previous one.

The carpenter who lived in this house used the first room to do extra work for private clients. Many of the tomb workers earned money in their spare time like this.

Men making furniture

Fire was started with a bow drill, some wood pierced with holes and a stick. The drill rotated the stick in a hole, causing friction and sparks.

The oven had a door at the bottom for raking the fire and opened at the top, where the cooked food was taken out.

The ancient Egyptians made many loaves and cakes. These men are cooking pancakes on a large flat stone over a fire.

This goatherd is churning goats' milk by swinging it to and fro in two skin bags as he walks along.

Beer was brewed by steeping barley dough in sweetened water and straining the fermented liquid into jars.

The men's eight-day working week (an Egyptian week had ten days) was often interrupted by one of the sixty or more festivals throughout the year.

There were festivals at the full moon, the beginning of spring, harvest time and at the river's flood. The villagers also joined in the 24-day festivities at Thebes in honour of the god Amun.

The village had its own festival in honour of a past pharaoh called Amenophis I, who was said to have founded the village and protected it.

EXCAVATING THE TOMB

A FTER THE FOUNDATION ceremony the workmen removed the surface sand and began tunnelling into the limestone hillside. They hollowed out an entrance corridor and flights of steps leading to chambers and store rooms. In some they left pillars of rock still standing to support the ceiling. Then they cut more steps, plunging deeper to the level where the pharaoh was to rest.

Soon the workers were beyond the reach of daylight. They worked by the light of hundreds of pottery oil lamps with wicks of twisted linen.

During the eight-day working week the men slept in a night camp, a group of huts close to the Valley of the Kings.

The two teams, known as the 'right side' team and the 'left side' team, worked on opposite sides of the tomb.

At midday, the men were allowed a break. They rested and ate a meal of bread, onions and beer.

The workmen were religious and prayed nightly. Their camp contained over 50 shrines to the gods.

After an evening meal that was usually made up of beans or boiled grain the exhausted workers slept at last.

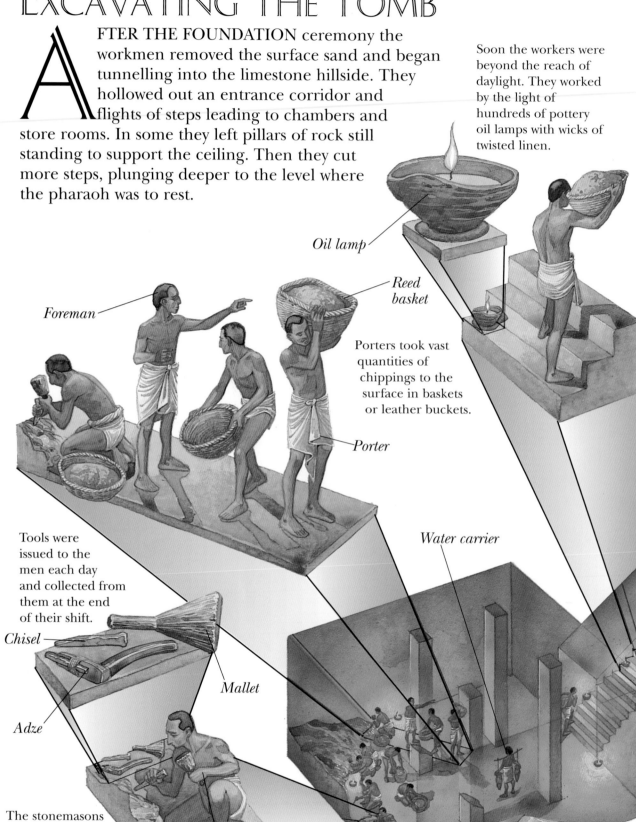

Oil lamp

Foreman

Reed basket

Porters took vast quantities of chippings to the surface in baskets or leather buckets.

Porter

Tools were issued to the men each day and collected from them at the end of their shift.

Chisel

Mallet

Adze

Water carrier

The stonemasons had only copper chisels and wooden mallets with which to hollow out the tomb's interior.

Stonemason

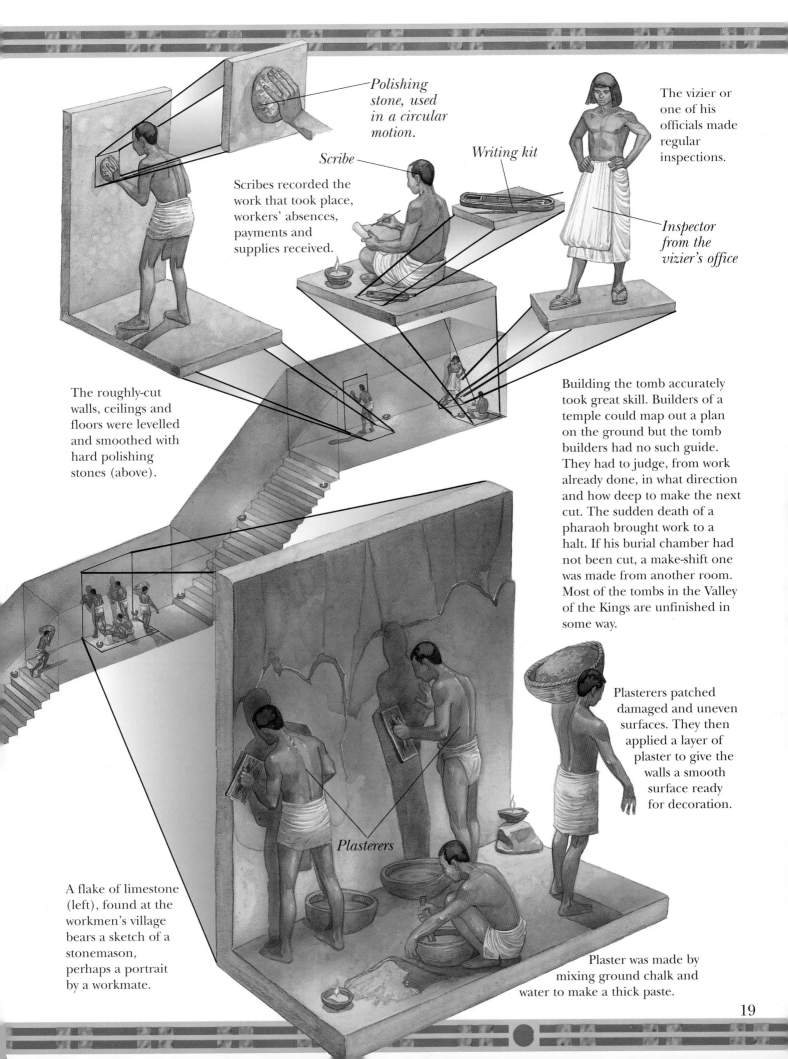

Polishing stone, used in a circular motion.

Scribe

Scribes recorded the work that took place, workers' absences, payments and supplies received.

Writing kit

The vizier or one of his officials made regular inspections.

Inspector from the vizier's office

The roughly-cut walls, ceilings and floors were levelled and smoothed with hard polishing stones (above).

Building the tomb accurately took great skill. Builders of a temple could map out a plan on the ground but the tomb builders had no such guide. They had to judge, from work already done, in what direction and how deep to make the next cut. The sudden death of a pharaoh brought work to a halt. If his burial chamber had not been cut, a make-shift one was made from another room. Most of the tombs in the Valley of the Kings are unfinished in some way.

Plasterers patched damaged and uneven surfaces. They then applied a layer of plaster to give the walls a smooth surface ready for decoration.

Plasterers

A flake of limestone (left), found at the workmen's village bears a sketch of a stonemason, perhaps a portrait by a workmate.

Plaster was made by mixing ground chalk and water to make a thick paste.

DECORATING THE WALLS

THE ANCIENT EGYPTIANS believed that the tomb was the entrance to a new life and they decorated its walls with scenes of the life to come. The tombs of ordinary people show them happily at work or at rest in the realm of Osiris. The royal tombs depict the stages of the sun god's journey through the sky by day and the underworld by night. People believed that in the next world the pharaoh would accompany the sun as it travelled beneath the earth to emerge next day in the east. The tomb artists did not need any powers of imagination to show these things. They drew them according to long-established rules.

Surfaces had to be carefully prepared, first with a chisel and then with a small adze that was held in the palm of the hand.

Before the final plastering, cracks in the rock face were filled with plaster. Large gaps were plugged with stone.

Sometimes the carver cut the figures into the wall instead of cutting out the background. This was a quicker method.

The reliefs were always painted. Many ancient Egyptian wall carvings seem plain now but they were originally very bright.

The reliefs could be cut into the plaster instead of the stone. This had to be done while the plaster was still damp.

THE PIGMENTS

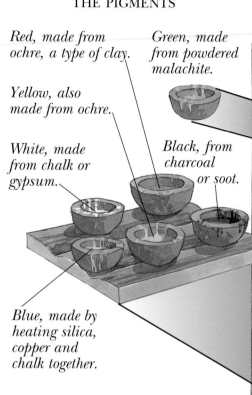

Red, made from ochre, a type of clay.

Green, made from powdered malachite.

Yellow, also made from ochre.

White, made from chalk or gypsum.

Black, from charcoal or soot.

Blue, made by heating silica, copper and chalk together.

Making paint

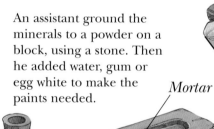

An assistant ground the minerals to a powder on a block, using a stone. Then he added water, gum or egg white to make the paints needed.

Mortar

Stone for grinding

An artist has practised upon this flake of stone (above), which was found in the Valley of the Kings. He has drawn Osiris.

This image of the goddess Isis (below), with her wings outstretched to protect the pharaoh, is found in many tombs.

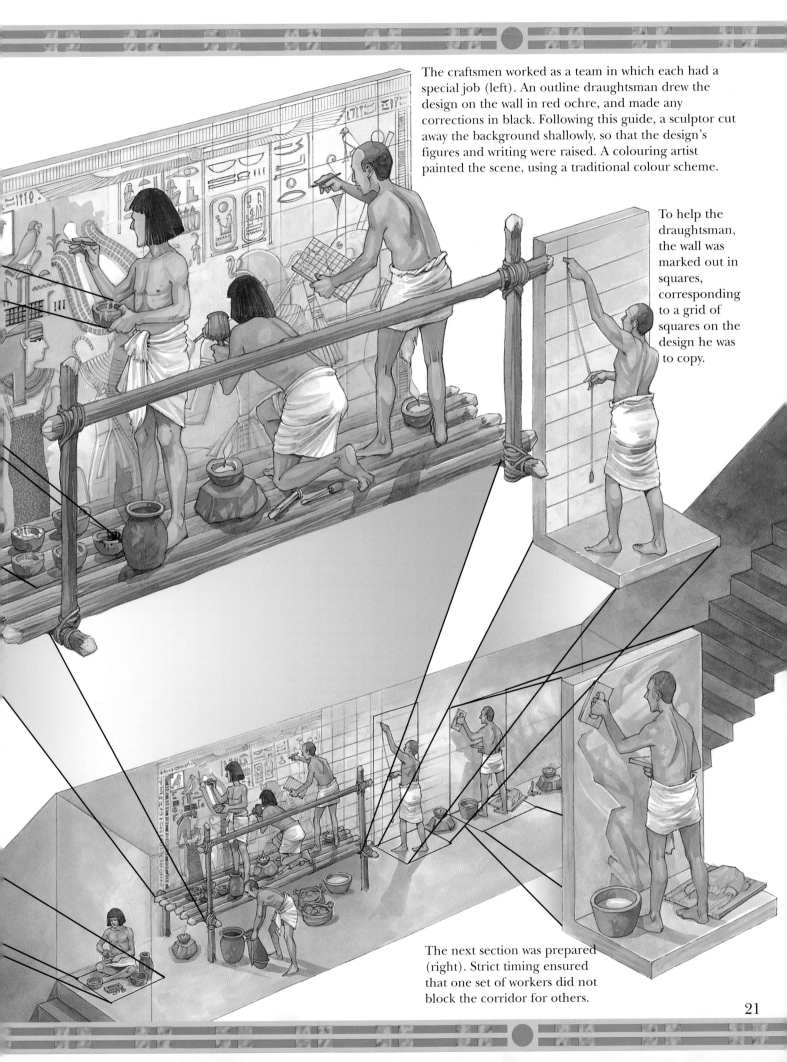

The craftsmen worked as a team in which each had a special job (left). An outline draughtsman drew the design on the wall in red ochre, and made any corrections in black. Following this guide, a sculptor cut away the background shallowly, so that the design's figures and writing were raised. A colouring artist painted the scene, using a traditional colour scheme.

To help the draughtsman, the wall was marked out in squares, corresponding to a grid of squares on the design he was to copy.

The next section was prepared (right). Strict timing ensured that one set of workers did not block the corridor for others.

MUMMIFICATION

WHEN A PHARAOH died, his tomb had to be ready to receive him after 70 days, which was the time it took to prepare his body for the afterlife. In the embalmers' workshop the body's internal organs were removed, it was dried out, treated with preservative oils and tightly wrapped in hundreds of metres of linen bandages. In this way, the pharaoh's body was turned into a mummy that would not decay. This was a sacred process, as the Egyptians believed they were copying the fate of Osiris who was mummified by Anubis and restored to immortal life.

First the body was dried out for 40 days in a vat packed with natron, a type of salt.

Protective amulets were placed in the mummy's wrappings.

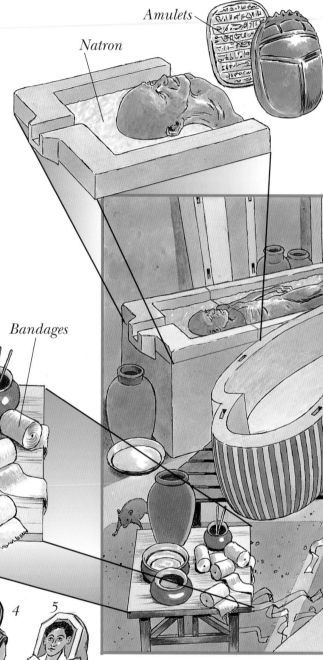

Amulets

Natron

Linen is a cloth woven from the fibres of the flax plant. Flax was harvested not by cutting it but by pulling it from the ground.

The flax stems were pulled through a wooden stripper to remove the seeds and then steeped in water until their fibres could be separated.

The fibres were beaten until they were soft. Then the spinners twisted them into strong thread, with the help of a spindle.

The linen was woven on a loom formed of two parallel beams pegged into the ground. The warp threads stretched between them.

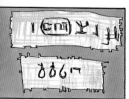

Linen ownership marks have been found on different mummies. The embalmers must have used second-hand cloth.

Palm wine, used to wash out and disinfect the inside of the body.

Bandages

Melted resin, which was poured into the head and the body cavity to prevent smells and decay.

Perfumed oil, which was massaged into the body to soften and perfume it.

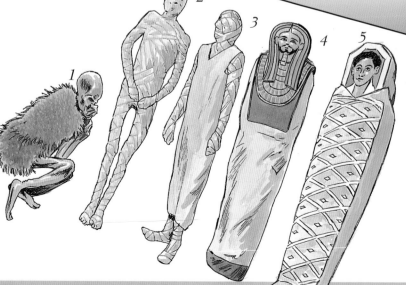

HOW WRAPPINGS CHANGED

1. Body in a goatskin (4000 BC).
2. Body coated in plaster-soaked linen (Old Kingdom).
3. Plaster-coated body wearing a linen dress (2500 BC).
4. Mummy with a mask covering head and chest (Middle Kingdom).
5. Elaborate bandaging (c. AD 100).

Amulets

The scarab amulet (far left, with a view of its base inscribed with a prayer) was placed over the heart. Many others, like the two on the left, were put between the bandages.

The ceremony of placing the mummy in its coffin was performed by a priest who was masked to represent Anubis, the god of mummification (right).

Women gathered lilies for making perfume. Scented juices were extracted from plants by crushing their leaves or petals.

Workers squeezed the juice from petals. To exert the maximum force, they would twist two rods passed through the ends of the bag.

The precious extracts were mixed with oil. Skilled oil blenders mingled flowers, crushed herbs and aromatic spices to make scents.

Scents made in this way could not keep their perfume for long. The most expensive were mixed with fat and stored in tiny ointment jars.

WRAPPING A MUMMY

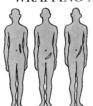

Before the body was dried, its internal organs were removed through a slit in the belly.

From the 21st dynasty onwards, the shape of the dried body was improved by stuffing it with plugs of linen.

First the head was bandaged, then the limbs and the torso. Linen pads were placed on the torso and legs and the mummy was bound spirally.

The mummy was wrapped in two linen shrouds and tied with cross-bandages. If a limb had rotted and fallen off, the embalmers made replacements from wads of linen.

Palm wine was a preservative. It was made from palm-tree sap, which was fermented and stored in sealed jars.

THE COFFIN MAKERS

WHILE MUMMIFICATION was taking place, in the royal workshops the most skilled carpenters in the land prepared the royal coffins. In New Kingdom times, very wealthy people had three coffins which fitted inside each other. Each of these was mummy-shaped, with a portrait of the person painted on it. The coffins of ordinary people were painted inside and out with prayers and pictures of the gods of death and rebirth. However, on the coffins of a pharaoh the decorations were not painted but finely carved and were covered entirely with gold.

The earliest burial containers were lidded baskets or large storage jars. The body was bent to fit inside it.

The first coffins were quite short, just big enough to take a bent up body. Plain, full-length coffins were in use by Old Kingdom times.

The finished carving was coated with a layer of gesso which was then covered with thin sheets of gold. (right). The eyes and other details were inlaid in coloured glass.

Sometimes delicate detail such as feathered wings were carved in a very thick layer of gesso.

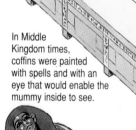

In Middle Kingdom times, coffins were painted with spells and with an eye that would enable the mummy inside to see.

Coffins shaped and painted to look like a masked mummy appeared in the Middle Kingdom, around 850 BC.

Royal coffins from the New Kingdom were carved with a pattern of feathers, as if the pharaoh had huge wings folded over his body.

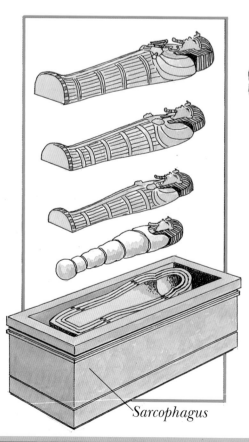

This picture (left) of a mummy and its three coffins shows how they nested, one inside the next. All three lay in a stone container called a sarcophagus.

Sarcophagus

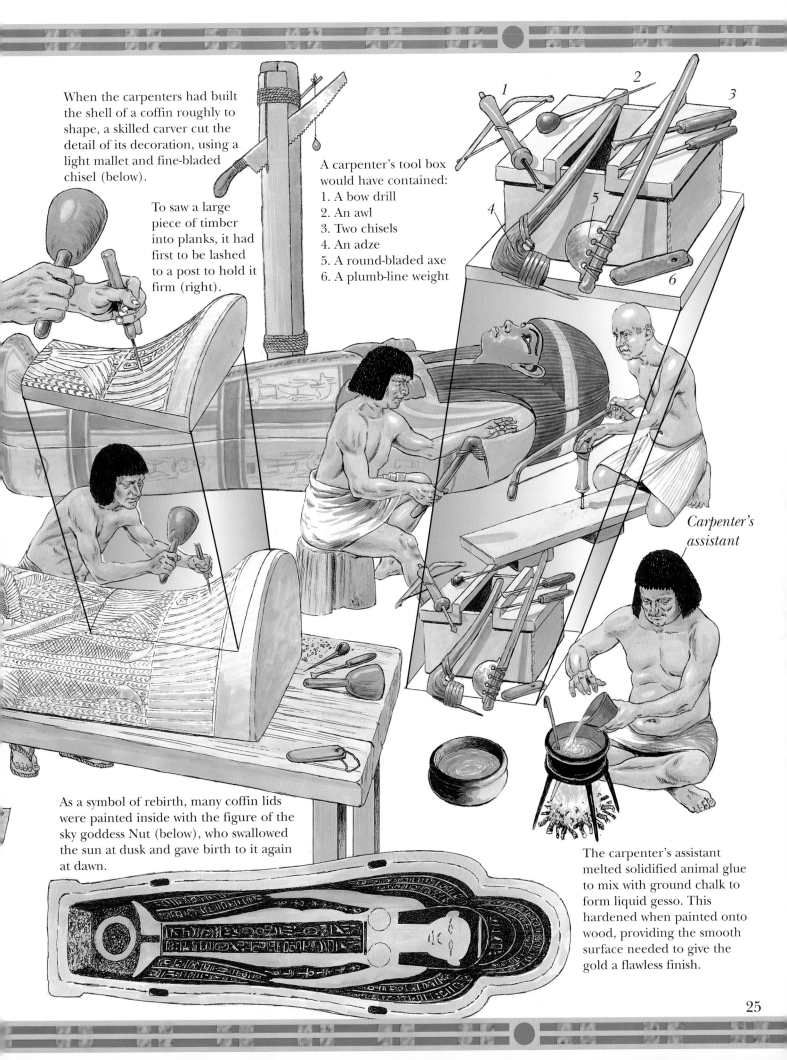

When the carpenters had built the shell of a coffin roughly to shape, a skilled carver cut the detail of its decoration, using a light mallet and fine-bladed chisel (below).

To saw a large piece of timber into planks, it had first to be lashed to a post to hold it firm (right).

A carpenter's tool box would have contained:
1. A bow drill
2. An awl
3. Two chisels
4. An adze
5. A round-bladed axe
6. A plumb-line weight

Carpenter's assistant

As a symbol of rebirth, many coffin lids were painted inside with the figure of the sky goddess Nut (below), who swallowed the sun at dusk and gave birth to it again at dawn.

The carpenter's assistant melted solidified animal glue to mix with ground chalk to form liquid gesso. This hardened when painted onto wood, providing the smooth surface needed to give the gold a flawless finish.

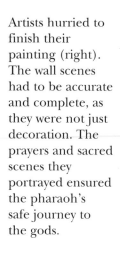

Artists hurried to finish their painting (right). The wall scenes had to be accurate and complete, as they were not just decoration. The prayers and sacred scenes they portrayed ensured the pharaoh's safe journey to the gods.

THE SARCOPHAGUS AND ITS SHRINES

I T WAS NOT UNUSUAL for work to be still going on in the pharaoh's burial chamber while his mummy was nearing completion and his funeral date had been fixed. The large stone sarcophagus that would hold the royal mummy and its coffins had to be ready to receive them. Stonemasons and sculptors worked on it in the burial chamber, since manoeuvring such a huge block of stone down the tomb's steps and passageways was a difficult task that had to be done long before the funeral day.

Antechamber

Storerooms

In the tomb of Tuthmosis III (c. 1425 BC) the sarcophagus was inscribed with sacred texts and images (above). A sculptor cut them into the red-painted quartzite, revealing its yellow colour, while a painter added touches of black and white.

Burial chamber

Royal sarcophagi with heavily sculpted lids appeared in the late 19th dynasty. The one on the left (c. 1160 BC) portrays Ramesses III in mummy form, with the goddesses Isis and Nephthys.

Well-loved pets were sometimes mummified and given sarcophagi. This one (left) belonged to a prince's pet cat and is made from limestone. Non-royal sarcophagi were usually made of wood.

Entrance

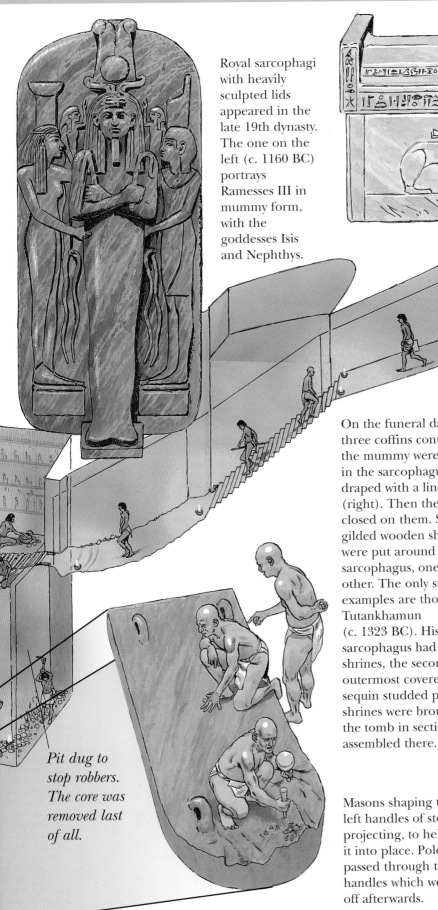

PUTTING UP THE SHRINES

On the funeral day the three coffins containing the mummy were placed in the sarcophagus and draped with a linen pall (right). Then the lid was closed on them. Several gilded wooden shrines were put around the sarcophagus, one over the other. The only surviving examples are those of Tutankhamun (c. 1323 BC). His sarcophagus had four shrines, the second-outermost covered with a sequin studded pall. The shrines were brought into the tomb in sections and assembled there.

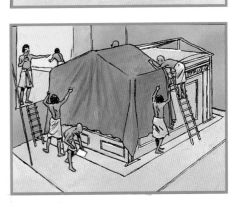

Pit dug to stop robbers. The core was removed last of all.

Masons shaping the lid left handles of stone projecting, to help to lift it into place. Poles were passed through the handles which were cut off afterwards.

27

THE CANOPIC JARS AND CHEST

BEFORE A BODY WAS MUMMIFIED its stomach, liver, lungs and intestines were removed because they would have made it rot. However, it was vital for these organs to be kept, as the entire body had to be preserved. They were therefore each dried separately, wrapped up and stored in a jar. The four jars, called canopic jars, were placed in a chest in the burial chamber, close to the mummy in its sarcophagus.

The earliest canopic chests were plain boxes of wood or stone, with compartments in which the four organs were put.

Another early custom was to store the four jars (one is cut away above to show contents) in a small pit cut in the burial chamber floor.

From Middle Kingdom times the jars were given human-headed lids to represent the four sons of the god Horus.

Above is a painted wooden canopic chest from about 1600 BC. It bears a picture of the embalming god, Anubis.

After about 1300 BC, it was usual for each jar's lid to have a different animal's head on it: a human's for the liver, a dog's for the stomach, a baboon's for the lungs and a falcon's for the intestines.

The canopic jars, in their chest, formed part of the procession that accompanied the mummy to its tomb. Below, Pharaoh Tutankhamun's canopic chest, housed in a large gilded shrine, is drawn along on a sled.

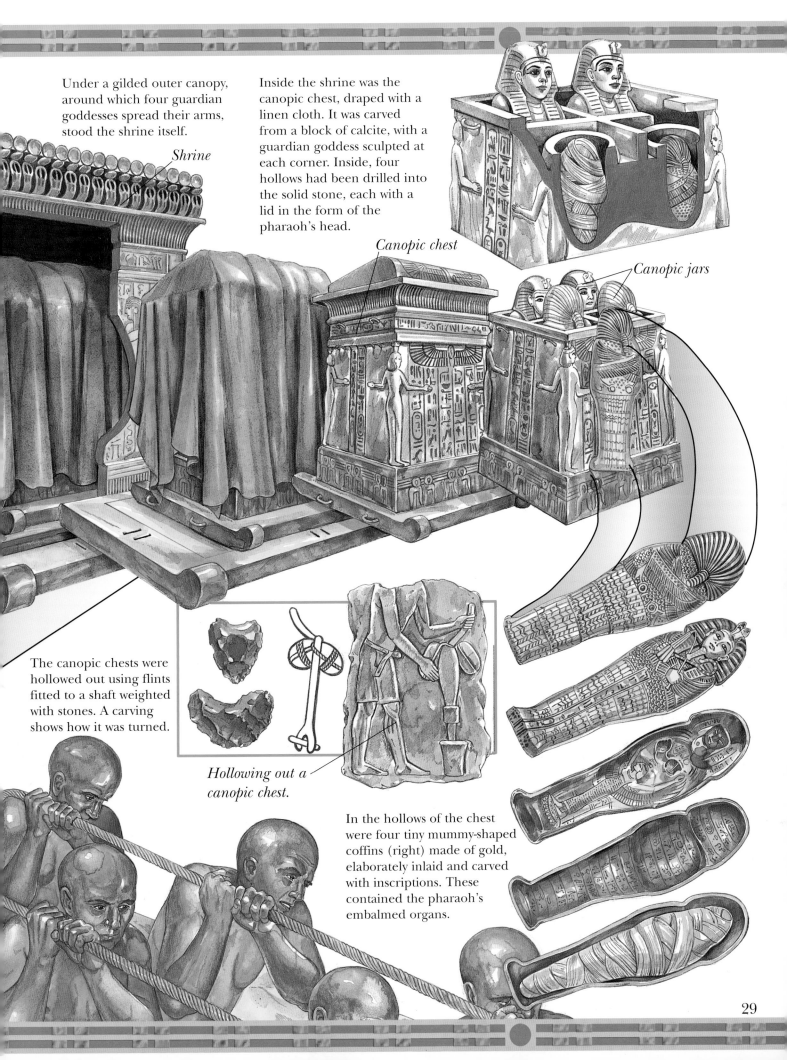

Under a gilded outer canopy, around which four guardian goddesses spread their arms, stood the shrine itself.

Shrine

Inside the shrine was the canopic chest, draped with a linen cloth. It was carved from a block of calcite, with a guardian goddess sculpted at each corner. Inside, four hollows had been drilled into the solid stone, each with a lid in the form of the pharaoh's head.

Canopic chest

Canopic jars

The canopic chests were hollowed out using flints fitted to a shaft weighted with stones. A carving shows how it was turned.

Hollowing out a canopic chest.

In the hollows of the chest were four tiny mummy-shaped coffins (right) made of gold, elaborately inlaid and carved with inscriptions. These contained the pharaoh's embalmed organs.

STOCKING THE TOMB

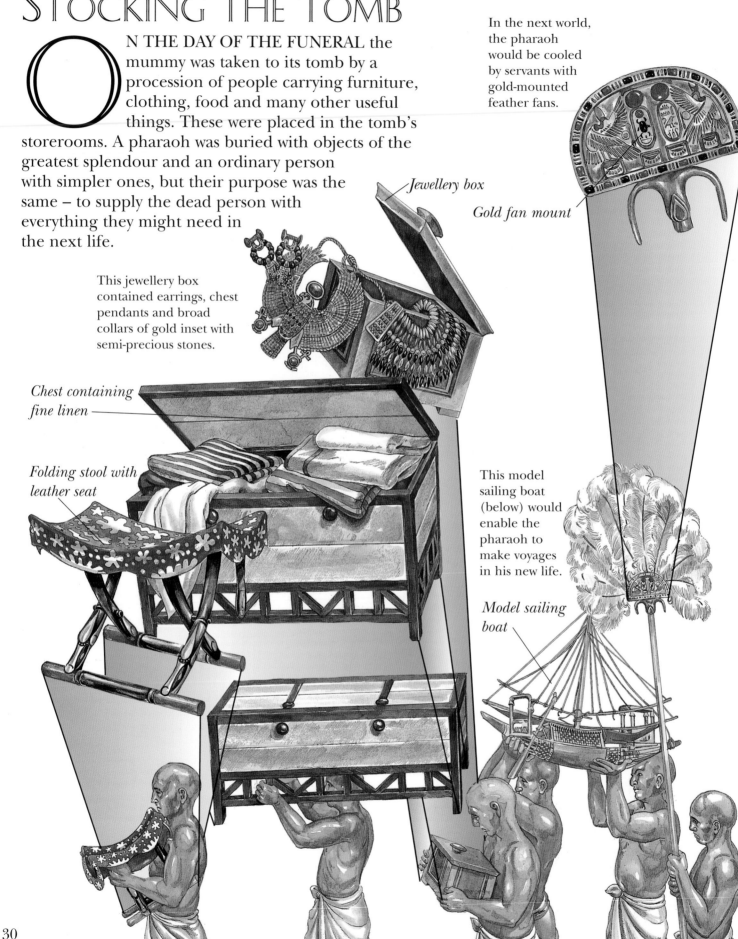

O N THE DAY OF THE FUNERAL the mummy was taken to its tomb by a procession of people carrying furniture, clothing, food and many other useful things. These were placed in the tomb's storerooms. A pharaoh was buried with objects of the greatest splendour and an ordinary person with simpler ones, but their purpose was the same – to supply the dead person with everything they might need in the next life.

In the next world, the pharaoh would be cooled by servants with gold-mounted feather fans.

This jewellery box contained earrings, chest pendants and broad collars of gold inset with semi-precious stones.

Jewellery box

Gold fan mount

Chest containing fine linen

Folding stool with leather seat

This model sailing boat (below) would enable the pharaoh to make voyages in his new life.

Model sailing boat

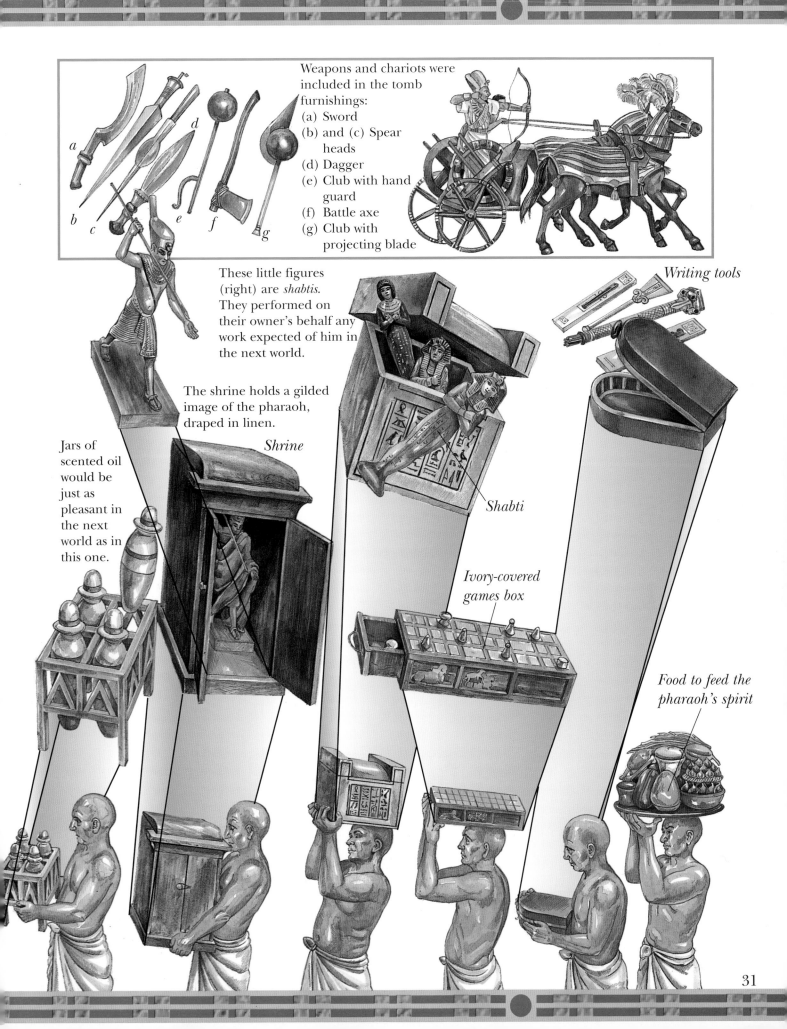

Weapons and chariots were included in the tomb furnishings:

(a) Sword
(b) and (c) Spear heads
(d) Dagger
(e) Club with hand guard
(f) Battle axe
(g) Club with projecting blade

a
b
c
d
e
f
g

These little figures (right) are *shabtis*. They performed on their owner's behalf any work expected of him in the next world.

The shrine holds a gilded image of the pharaoh, draped in linen.

Writing tools

Shrine

Shabti

Jars of scented oil would be just as pleasant in the next world as in this one.

Ivory-covered games box

Food to feed the pharaoh's spirit

PHARAOH JOINS THE GODS

ON HIS FUNERAL DAY the pharaoh made his last journey in this world, across the Nile to the western bank where the dead rested in their tombs. His own tomb waited to receive him there. His body was accompanied by his successor, the new pharaoh, together with his royal relatives, courtiers, high officials and priests. After them came a long line of bearers carrying furniture and provisions for the tomb. At the tomb's entrance, the procession halted and the mummy was set upright for the Opening of the Mouth, a ceremony that magically reawakened the dead pharaoh's senses, so that he was ready for his new life.

The dead pharaoh's queen and chief courtiers (right) watched in silence as the last ceremony, that enabled him to begin his new life, was performed.

Women dressed in blue mourning robes wailed and threw dust upon their heads as signs of grief. They were professional mourners hired to give public expression to everyone's sorrow.

Bearers

Canopic shrine

Mourners

Funeral bier

THE PHARAOH MAKES HIS LAST JOURNEY

Two royal women said prayers of rebirth over the pharaoh's mummy. They were representing Isis and her sister, who had brought Osiris to life.

When the priests took the mummy away for its funeral, the women played the roles of frantic mourners and made ritual attempts to stop them.

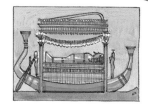

For its journey to the tomb the mummy was set on a boat-shaped bier which was mounted on a sledge so that it could be pulled along.

The mummy went by boat across the Nile and along a canal to its mortuary temple. After rituals here it was taken to the Valley of the Kings.

A small party descended to the burial chamber. Before the sarcophagus was sealed the queen placed a collar of flowers round the coffin neck.

The two viziers were in attendance.

Viziers

This copy of a tomb painting shows a pharaoh's garlanded funeral bier being drawn along by priests with white mourning bands around their heads.

Ritual implements (left), including a double-bladed knife, an adze and flasks of oil, were used in the ceremony.

Opening of the Mouth

A priest wearing the mask of Anubis held the mummy upright (above). The new pharaoh, dressed in the leopard skin worn by priests, performed the Opening of the Mouth ceremony.

Throughout the ceremony priests burned incense and recited sacred prayers (left).

In this scene the dead pharaoh, with his _ka_, is greeted by Osiris, while on the right his successor performs the Opening of the Mouth on his mummy.

This scene shows the pharaoh being welcomed to the afterlife by Hathor, who touches his mouth with the symbol of life. Anubis stands behind him.

When the gilded shrines had been set up and the funeral goods put in place, the last priest to leave swept the floor clear of all footprints.

After the burial ceremony a funeral feast was held close to the tomb. The guests wore collars of flowers around their necks.

REDISCOVERING THE TOMBS

FROM THE END of the New Kingdom, the Valley of the Kings was no longer used for royal burials. In time, sand and falling rock buried most of the tombs. A few stood open and were admired by ancient Greek and Roman visitors, but over the following centuries their history and meaning were forgotten. Little was known of the valley until archeologists began work there in the 19th century. Each of them hoped to find a tomb that still held all its burial goods, but all were disappointed. Then, in 1922, a discovery was made that stunned the world – a royal tomb packed with priceless treasures was found.

Below is the tomb of Tutankhamun, showing in time-slices how it was lost and rediscovered.

The mummy was examined in 1925, and again in 1968, to see what clues it held to the life and death of the pharaoh. It was discovered that he was about seventeen when he died.

Storerooms, containing gilded furniture, chariots and chests.

The mummy lay in an inner coffin of solid gold.

The entrance, packed with rubble in ancient times.

The stairs, also filled. Carter had to dig his way in.

1925

Carter and his team spent nearly ten years working in the tomb. Each object was numbered, photographed and carefully described before being sent to Cairo for preservation and safekeeping.

1922

Archaeologist Howard Carter (far left) made the find. He and his patron Lord Carnarvon (centre, with his daughter) were the first to enter.

When Carter started digging, he was working on a hunch. Some years earlier a cup bearing the name of Tutankhamun had been found in the area along with objects used in his burial (right).

Natron in linen bag

Pottery jar

Faience jar

Collar of flowers and beads

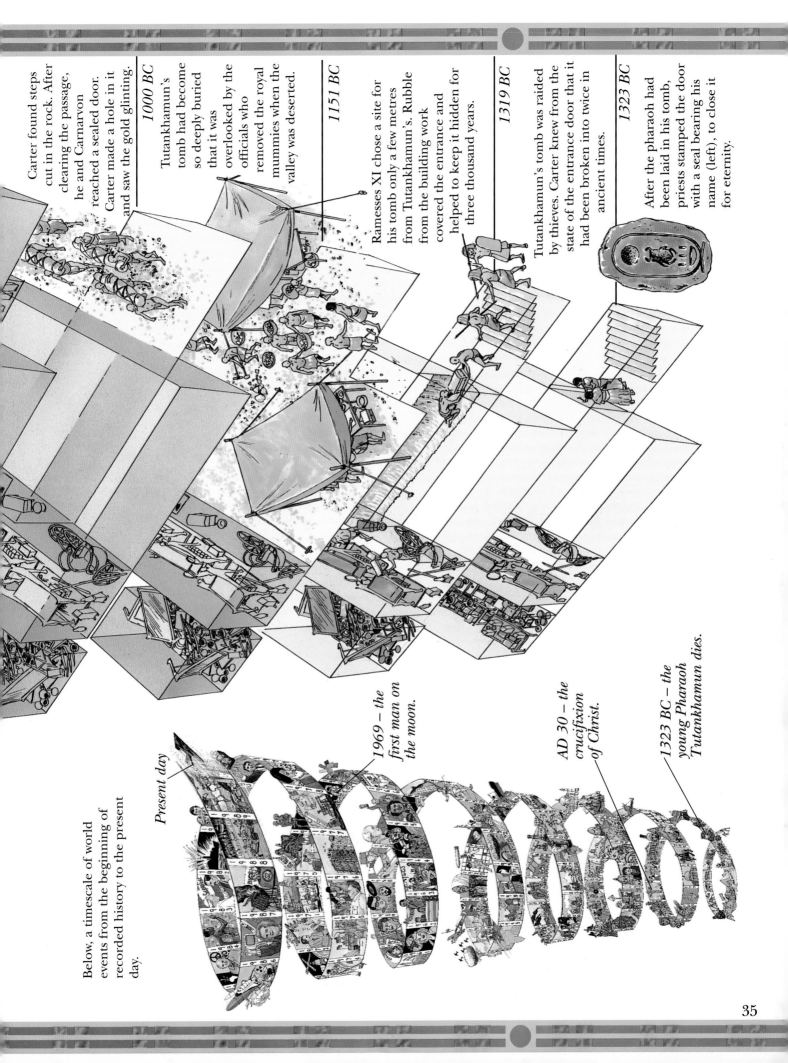

Carter found steps cut in the rock. After clearing the passage, he and Carnarvon reached a sealed door. Carter made a hole in it and saw the gold glinting.

1000 BC

Tutankhamun's tomb had become so deeply buried that it was overlooked by the officials who removed the royal mummies when the valley was deserted.

1151 BC

Ramesses XI chose a site for his tomb only a few metres from Tutankhamun's. Rubble from the building work covered the entrance and helped to keep it hidden for three thousand years.

1319 BC

Tutankhamun's tomb was raided by thieves. Carter knew from the state of the entrance door that it had been broken into twice in ancient times.

1323 BC

After the pharaoh had been laid in his tomb, priests stamped the door with a seal bearing his name (left), to close it for eternity.

Below, a timescale of world events from the beginning of recorded history to the present day.

Present day

1969 – the first man on the moon.

AD 30 – the crucifixion of Christ.

1323 BC – the young Pharaoh Tutankhamun dies.

WHO WAS TUTANKHAMUN?

TODAY, everyone interested in ancient Egypt has heard of Tutankhamun. Through the survival of his tomb, full of treasures, he has become Egypt's most famous pharaoh. Yet in his own time he was not an important ruler and very little is known about him. He came to the throne as a small boy when Egypt was in a state of upheaval. The priests were angry and the people confused because the previous pharaoh, Tutankhamun's father, Akhnaten, had forced them to give up their traditional gods and only worship Aten, the sun disk. Interested only in religious ideas, Akhnaten had failed to govern the country well.

Like all royal babies, Tutankhamun would have been cared for by a wet nurse (a servant with breast milk to spare).

While they were small, royal princes lived in a special part of the palace reserved for the royal women and their servants.

Tutankhamun was not free to enjoy himself like an ordinary boy, but bird hunting in the marshes was a suitable royal sport.

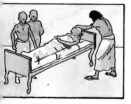

Tutankhamun's older half-brother, Smenkhkare, would have been the next pharaoh, if he had not died at about the same time as their father.

This solid gold portrait mask of Tutankhamun covered the head of his mummy.

Below is Tutankhamun's family tree. Akhnaten, like most pharaohs, had a chief wife and several minor ones. Tutankhamun's mother was a minor wife.

Amenophis III

Queen Tye

Queen Nefertiti

Kiya, a minor wife of Akhnaten.

Amenophis IV, who changed his name to Akhnaten.

Smenkhkare, who may have ruled jointly with his father for a time.

Ankhesenamun

Tutankhamun

Judging from his mummy, Tutankhamun was aged about seventeen when he died. He is known to have reigned for roughly nine years, so he must have become god-king of all Egypt when he was only seven or eight years old.

His bride was his half-sister, Ankhesenamun.

The young ruler wore a crown and carried emblems (the crook and flail) that symbolised his power.

Ay, the head of the cavalry, and Horemheb, the army chief, both tried to influence their young pharaoh.

The royal advisors hastened to undo Akhnaten's religious reforms. The temples were reopened.

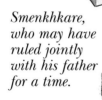

Akhnaten

Nefertiti

To judge from her portrait bust (right), Akhnaten's chief wife, Queen Nefertiti, was very beautiful. She shared her husband's religious views.

A stone carving (left), shows Akhnaten and Nefertiti receiving the blessing of Aten, who is represented as a disk of light. The couple are nursing their children just as they might at home (below).

Tutankhamun's mummy, unwrapped in 1925, has a head wound near the left ear. This has given rise to the theory that he was murdered.

But perhaps the blow was accidental? Or the king could have had a fatal illness and the injury could have been caused during embalming.

Akhnaten built a new capital city, which he named Akhtaten in honour of his god. The house below is a reconstruction of one of its buildings.

Queen Nefertiti

Tutankhamun had no heir. Many people could have been hoping to be pharaoh. His unexpected death must have caused all sorts of rumours.

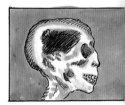

Tutankhamun, too young to know how to rule effectively, was controlled by his advisors. It has been suggested that one of them engineered his death, though there is no proof of this. He died before there had been time to build him a royal tomb and was buried in a much smaller one, originally meant for someone else.

X-rays show a misplaced fragment of bone inside Tutankhamun's skull. Was this due to injury before or after death? No one knows.

The pharaoh's name was changed from Tutankhaten (living image of Aten) to Tutankhamun (living image of Amun).

Tutankhamun's two babies were both dead at birth. Their mummies were found in Tutankhamun's tomb.

The city that Akhnaten had created was abandoned and the pharaoh's government moved to Memphis.

Tutankhamun's death would have been mourned with the customary show of grief, but for some people it may have been convenient. It has been suggested that he might have been trying to shed his advisors and make his own decisions.

Ay became the next pharaoh. He ruled for only four years. Next on the throne was Horemheb.

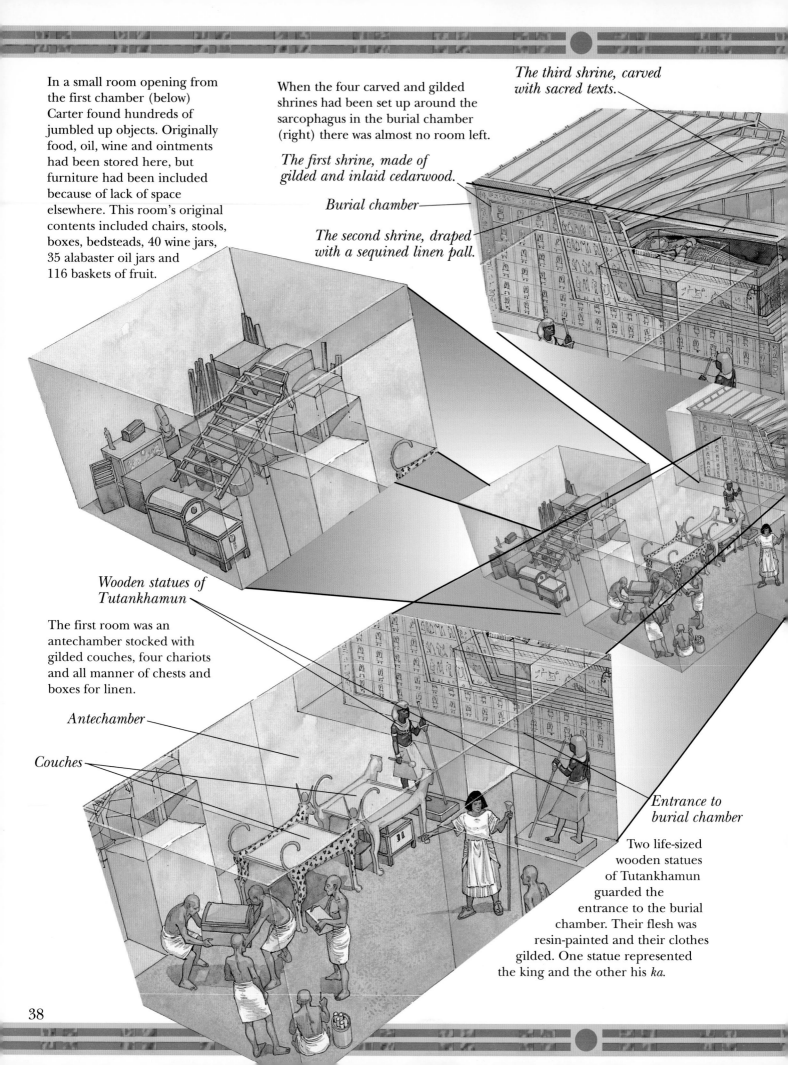

In a small room opening from the first chamber (below) Carter found hundreds of jumbled up objects. Originally food, oil, wine and ointments had been stored here, but furniture had been included because of lack of space elsewhere. This room's original contents included chairs, stools, boxes, bedsteads, 40 wine jars, 35 alabaster oil jars and 116 baskets of fruit.

When the four carved and gilded shrines had been set up around the sarcophagus in the burial chamber (right) there was almost no room left.

The first shrine, made of gilded and inlaid cedarwood.

Burial chamber

The second shrine, draped with a sequined linen pall.

The third shrine, carved with sacred texts.

Wooden statues of Tutankhamun

The first room was an antechamber stocked with gilded couches, four chariots and all manner of chests and boxes for linen.

Antechamber

Couches

Entrance to burial chamber

Two life-sized wooden statues of Tutankhamun guarded the entrance to the burial chamber. Their flesh was resin-painted and their clothes gilded. One statue represented the king and the other his *ka*.

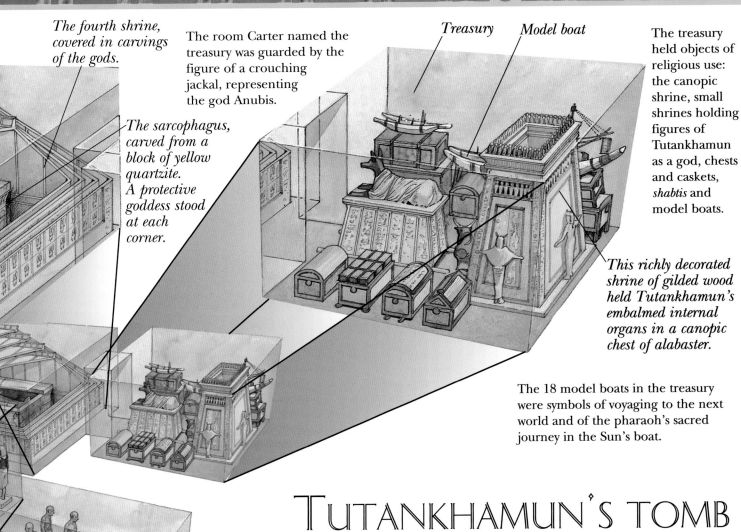

The fourth shrine, covered in carvings of the gods.

The room Carter named the treasury was guarded by the figure of a crouching jackal, representing the god Anubis.

The sarcophagus, carved from a block of yellow quartzite. A protective goddess stood at each corner.

Treasury   Model boat

The treasury held objects of religious use: the canopic shrine, small shrines holding figures of Tutankhamun as a god, chests and caskets, *shabtis* and model boats.

This richly decorated shrine of gilded wood held Tutankhamun's embalmed internal organs in a canopic chest of alabaster.

The 18 model boats in the treasury were symbols of voyaging to the next world and of the pharaoh's sacred journey in the Sun's boat.

As porters carried Tutankhamun's funeral goods into his tomb (above), a superintendent showed where they must be put. Stocking this tomb was an awkward job as there was little space for all the things a pharaoh needed. In a normal New Kingdom royal burial there would have been several pillared halls and storerooms to fill.

TUTANKHAMUN'S TOMB

WHEN HOWARD CARTER and Lord Carnarvon dug their way into Tutankhamun's tomb they were dazzled by the riches it held. Although it had been robbed in ancient times, the thieves had only taken things that they could carry easily. The burial chamber was untouched. Its gilded shrines still enclosed the massive sarcophagus in which the pharaoh lay, in an innermost coffin of solid gold weighing 110.4 kg. Magnificent jewellery adorned the mummy, which wore a headpiece of heavy beaten gold, inlaid with lapis lazuli. The storerooms held gilded thrones, furniture and splendid caskets of ivory and wood, painted with scenes or inlaid with gold and with blue faience. There were lamps, precious vessels and toilet objects, all of exquisite workmanship. Yet these were the grave goods of a young and unimportant pharaoh, hastily buried in a makeshift tomb with little storage space. Imagine the wealth that once lay piled in the great royal tombs!

ROBBING THE TOMB

DESPITE THE SACRED nature of the tombs they were often looted, sometimes not long after the funeral. Records reveal that the culprits were often the tomb builders themselves. The robbers of Tutankhamun's tomb knew its layout well – they went straight to the jewellery chests in the treasury. If they had not been caught, they would almost certainly have returned and done far more damage. As it is, the tomb's contents (now in Cairo museum) are one of the wonders of the world.

A successful robbery had to be carefully planned. Several people had to cooperate, some to do the tunnelling, others to be look-outs.

By a prearranged deal with a ferryman, the goods could be got across across the river fast, in case suspects' houses were searched.

Police checked the tomb doors regularly for signs of a break-in, but robbers could outwit them by tunnelling in from above.

When the valley police inspected the doors and found the official seal on them unbroken they assumed that all was well.

Someone opened the doors of the first big shrine (left) but went no further. The robbers wanted things that were easy to carry.

Fine linen was valuable. That is what this thief (right) is after, while his companion sniffs a jar of perfumed oil to see if it is still good.

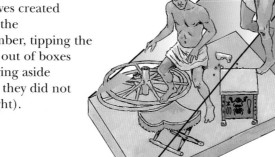

The thieves created chaos in the antechamber, tipping the contents out of boxes and flinging aside anything they did not want (right).

A thief dropped eight gold rings tied in a scarf (above) and someone tossed it back into the tomb.

What the robbers most wanted was gold. They smashed open shrines and hacked them to pieces to strip off the gilding.

They prised off the lids of sarcophagi – not an easy job as many lids had a locking device – but well worth it to get at the contents.

They smashed up coffins in order to detach their gold coverings and slit open the mummy wrappings to reach the jewellery inside.

Chests and coffers were forced open and ransacked to discover their contents. The thieves were looking for jewellery and linen.

Marks on the walls of certain tombs show that robbers would hurl smaller things against them, to smash the object and detach its gold.

The tomb was robbed at least twice. The second gang had to dig its way through the rubble which had been used to block the passage when the first break-in was discovered (left).

The robbers knew where to look. They did not bother to open shrines holding wooden statues but ransacked the boxes of jewellery (left).

It seems, from objects they hurriedly dropped, that the robbers were surprised by the valley police. Officials made a quick rough job of tidying the tomb and reblocked the passage.

Police

The door of the tomb was resealed with the official stamp – a jackal and nine captives (right).

For most of the valley's history its police kept a sharp eye on the tombs. Robbers caught red-handed were marched to the vizier.

The vizier started an inquiry. He sent inspectors to the valley to make reports and had all suspects rounded up for questioning.

The records of some of these trials have survived. If people were reluctant to give evidence they were beaten until they answered.

This hieroglyph meaning 'punishment' suggests that convicted robbers were impaled on a stake.

Another way of getting at the gold was to set fire to everything and return later to scrape hardened pools of gold from beneath the ash.

Buyers in Thebes did not ask awkward questions when offered a bargain.

By the end of the New Kingdom valley security had grown so poor that it became official policy to clear out raided tombs.

Officials would remove the royal mummy and strip the tomb of its remaining assets. Any precious metals went to help the state's finances.

The battered mummies were rewrapped and hidden away together in a few easily guarded tombs.

TIMESPAN

The history of ancient Egypt spans over three thousand years. To make this immense length of time easier to grasp, historians have divided it into three long periods (called the Old, the Middle and New Kingdoms). During these times, Egypt was united and prosperous. The three Kingdoms are separated by times of confusion (the Intermediate Periods) when there was civil war and foreign invasions of Egypt. Finally there is the Late Period, when Egypt was in decline. The timeline pictured below shows when the different periods in Egypt's long history started and finished and shows when the pyramids and tombs were built.

Official stamp, used to seal the tomb doors

A carving of Osiris

Egypt's pharaohs, of which about 250 are recorded, are grouped into dynasties. A dynasty is a succession of rulers belonging to related families. While thirty two dynasties came and went (over a period more than one and a half times longer than that which separates us from the ancient Romans!), the Egyptian way of life hardly changed at all. The people's faith in their pharaoh and the gods, their attitude to life and death and their trust in the living tomb remained the same at all times.

The Archaic period In prehistoric times there were many small chiefdoms along the Nile valley. In time, these formed two major kingdoms –

Upper and Lower Egypt. Egypt's recorded history began in about 3100 BC when the two kingdoms were united by a warrior called Menes. He became the first pharaoh of all Egypt.

During this period, graves were covered by mounds. These later developed a flat, straight-sided shape which resembled a house. In much more recent times, the Arabs, thinking they looked bench-shaped, called these mounds 'mastabas' –

Amulets

their word for bench – and this name has stuck.

The Old Kingdom (2682-2181 BC – 3rd-8th dynasties) During this period of peace and stability, the first pyramids were built, to provide the pharaohs with everlasting tombs. The most famous are the three at Giza:

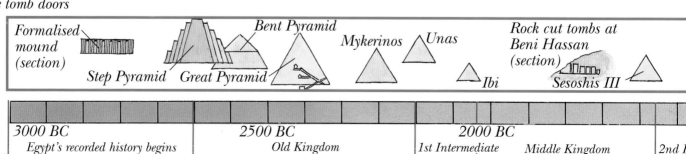

| Formalised mound (section) | Step Pyramid | Great Pyramid | Bent Pyramid | Mykerinos | Unas | Ibi | Rock cut tombs at Beni Hassan (section) | Sesoshis III |

| 3000 BC | | 2500 BC | | 2000 BC | |
| Egypt's recorded history begins | | Old Kingdom | | 1st Intermediate Period | Middle Kingdom | 2nd Intermediate Period |

Isis

the Great Pyramid, built c. 2550 BC for Kheops, a pharaoh of the 4th dynasty, and the pyramids of his son Khephren and of Khephren's successor Mykerinos. The great Sphinx, an enormous man-headed lion at the approach to Khephren's pyramid also dates from this time.

First Intermediate period (2181-2040 BC – 9th-11th dynasties)
The authority of the pharaohs weakened. Egypt split into two warring kingdoms, one in the north and one in the south.

Middle Kingdom (2040-1786 BC – 11th-14th dynasties)
A prince from the city of Thebes united the country and a second great age began. Egypt's prosperity and military strength increased. Pyramids continued to be built but they were on a smaller scale and were made from mud brick. Impressive private tombs were cut into the hillside overlooking the Nile in middle Egypt.

Second Intermediate Period (1786-1567 BC – 15th-17th dynasties)
Asiatic invaders, called the Hyksos, invaded lower Egypt.

Tutankhamun's death mask

New Kingdom (1567-1085 BC – 18th-20th dynasties)
The leaders of upper Egypt defeated the Hyksos and reunited the kingdom. Under famous pharaohs, such as Tuthmosis III and the war-like Ramesses II, Egypt was at the peak of her prosperity at home and her fame abroad. Tutankhamun made his brief appearance in the 18th dynasty and the great temples at modern Karnak and Luxor (Thebes) were built. This is the period of the rock-cut royal tombs in the Valley of the Kings.

Third Intermediate Period (1085-712 BC – 21st-24th dynasties)
Egypt's prosperity declined. Under weak rulers the country was attacked by one enemy after another.

Late Period (712-332 BC – 25th-31st dynasties)
During this time Egypt was conquered by the Persians.

Greco-Roman period (332 BC-AD 395)
Alexander the Great drove out the Persians and put Greek pharaohs on the throne. In 30 BC Egypt became a province of the Roman Empire.

Queen Nefertiti

Amenophis II (plan) *Rock cut tomb of Ahmose (section)* *Ramesses IV (section)*

Ancient Greece 850 BC-140 BC

Ancient Rome 753 BC-AD 476

1000 BC   *500 BC*

diate   New Kingdom   3rd Intermediate Period   Late Period

GLOSSARY

Adze A tool used for trimming wood, which had a blade set at right angles to the handle.

Alabaster A type of fine, translucent and veined limestone used by the Egyptians in architecture. It was often used to make sarcophagi.

Amulet A small object, either worn or carried on one's person, which was thought to ward off evil.

Awl A tool used to pierce holes.

Bow drill A drill encircled by the string of a small bow. The bow was pushed back and forth, causing the string to rotate the drill.

Calcite A crystallised form of chalk.

Causeway A raised roadway built on an embankment.

Embalmers People whose trade is the preserving of dead bodies with spices and oils before the funeral.

Faience Decoration made from glazed powdered quartz.

Flail A tool with a heavy wooden club, hinged to swing freely from a long handle. It was carried by the pharaoh to symbolise kingship.

Funeral bier A moveable frame on which a coffin is placed so that it can be taken to its grave or tomb.

Gesso A mixture of ground up chalk and glue which was applied to wood to give it a smooth surface, ready for painting or gilding.

Gypsum A white powdery mineral.

Hieroglyph A picture sign. These signs, which could represent either objects or sounds, formed the ancient Egyptian alphabet.

Incense A mixture of gums or spices that produce a sweet smell when burnt.

Ka One of the aspects of a person's immortal spirit, according to the ancient Egyptians. They believed that it was a spiritual double of the living person, and that it would live on after death, if nourished.

Lapis lazuli A dark blue semi-precious stone.

Litter A seat or couch mounted on horizontal poles, in which a person could be carried. The poles rested on the bearers' shoulders.

Lector priest A priest whose job it was to read out sacred verses and prayers during religious ceremonies.

Malachite A green-coloured mineral.

Mortuary temple A temple in which rites were performed to secure the well-being of the dead. Pyramids had mortuary temples attached to them. As this was not possible in the narrow Valley of the Kings, New Kingdom mortuary temples were some distance from their tombs.

Natron A natural form of salt, used in ancient Egyptian purification and mummification techniques.

Ochre A type of clay containing oxide of iron which gives it a colour varying from yellow to brownish red.

Pall A cloth that was draped over the coffin.

Plumb-line weight A stone or lead weight which is attached to a piece of thread. When the weight is allowed to hang freely the thread provides a true vertical line.

Porters Tomb workers whose job it was to carry stone and rubble back up to the surface.

Quartzite A very hard rock, with a yellowish colour. Ancient Egyptians sometimes used it to build their sarcophagi.

Resin The sweet-smelling sap that oozes from fir and pine trees.

Sarcophagus (pl. sarcophagi) An outermost stone coffin which in ancient Egyptian times held one or more wooden coffins and was often covered in carvings.

Scribe A professional writer, responsible for all official reports.

Sequin A small metal disk sewn onto cloth as decoration.

Shabtis Small figurines, placed in tombs, to ensure that the tomb owner would not have to work in the next world. If any unpleasant duties were expected of him, the *shabtis* would perform them on his behalf.

Shrine A cupboard-like container, made of wood or metal, in which the image of a god was kept.

Shroud A cloth in which a body is wrapped for burial.

Silica A mineral substance found, in the form of quartz, in many rocks.

Underworld A place beneath the earth, which the ancient Egyptians believed was full of hidden dangers. After death, they had to find their way through the underworld safely, with the help of spells and prayers, before they could enter the afterlife.

Vizier A ruler's chief minister. Egypt originally had one vizier but in New Kingdom times there were two – one for the north and one for the south of the country.

INDEX

Page numbers in **bold** refer to illustrations

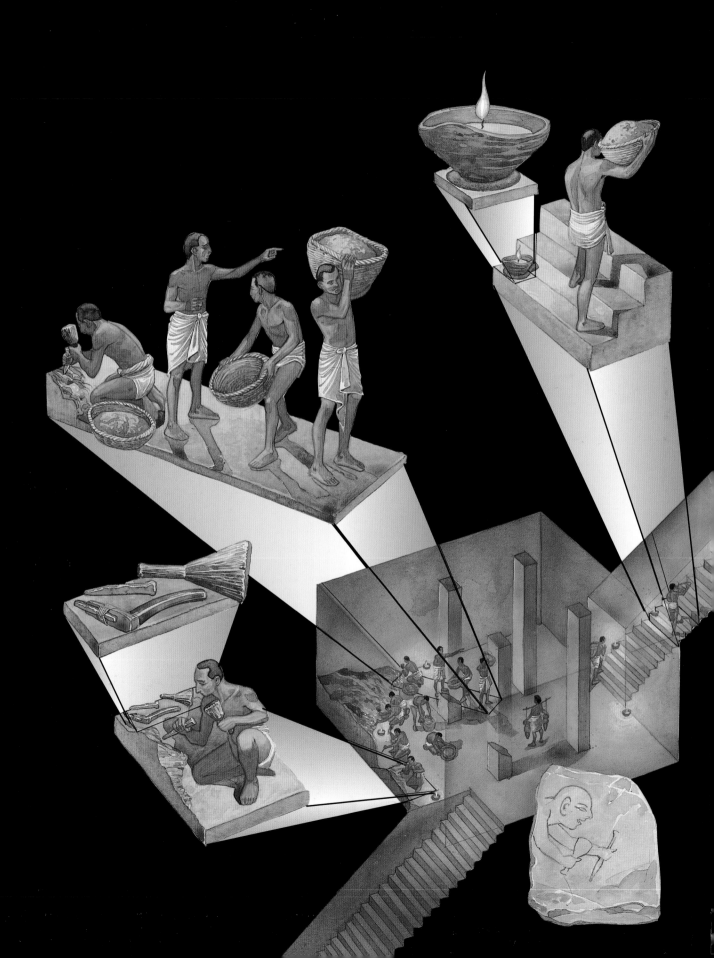